French
Revision

Gill James

Good day. I'm Sir Ralph Witherbottom. I'm an accomplished inventor, a dashing discoverer and an enthusiastic entrepreneur.

Hi! I'm Isabella Witherbottom – my friends call me Izzy. I'm Sir Ralph's daughter and I like to keep him on his toes!

And they both keep me on my toes! How do you do? I'm Max, the butler, at your service.

Woof! I'm Spotless – aptly named, as you can see. I'm the family's loyal dog.

Contents

Hello, hello, hello!
Allô, allô, allô!

Sir Ralph Witherbottom got into a complete pickle on his first day in his new house in France. He said, '**Bonne nuit**' to the cook first thing in the morning. "That means, 'good night'," whispered Max, the butler. "You mean, '**Bonjour**'."

The housekeeper gave him a funny look when he said, '**Salut**', as he kissed her hand. "You should only use that when you're talking to people you know really well," explained Max, the butler.

Sir Ralph shouted, '**Allô**!' at the small boy, who was delivering groceries from the nearby village.

"Papa, you should only say that when you're answering the phone," said Isabella Witherbottom. "You mean, 'Bonjour'."

When the boy waved goodbye, Isabella called after him, '**À bientôt**'. Sir Ralph looked puzzled. "It means, 'see you soon'," explained Isabella.

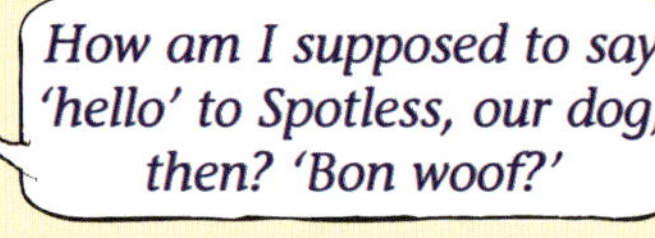

When the people from next door popped by that evening to welcome their new neighbours, Sir Ralph opened the door and said, '**Au revoir**'.

"Sir, that means 'goodbye'," whispered Max. "I think you mean, '**Bonsoir**'!"

Say the right thing

Match the greeting with the picture. The first one has been done for you.

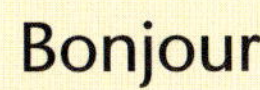

Bonjour

Bonsoir

À bientôt

Salut

Allô

Au revoir

Bonne nuit

Top Tips!

You use 'bon' for **masculine** parts of the day, e.g. 'soir', and 'bonne' for **feminine** ones, e.g. 'nuit'.

Did you know?

'**Bonne journée**' is a simple way of saying, 'Have a nice day!' You can also use '**Bonne soirée**' in a similar way to mean, 'Have a nice evening!' You might use either of these phrases when someone is going out for the day or evening. You use 'bonjour' or 'bonsoir' when you first see them again.

How's it going, my little one?
Ça va, mon petit chou?

Sir Ralph Witherbottom was scratching his head and looking puzzled.

"We saw the old lady from the house next door while we were out for our walk. She made a fuss of Spotless and said, '**Ça va, mon petit chou?**' Doesn't that mean, 'How are you, my little cabbage?'"

"Yes, that's right," said Max, the butler. "It's like us saying, 'How are you, my little one?' What did she say to you, though?"

"Oh, '**Comment allez-vous, Monsieur** Witherbottom?' of course," answered Sir Ralph. "I replied, '**Très bien, merci, et vous?**'. You see, I know how to be polite to old ladies."

"I'm pleased to hear it, sir," replied Max. "Of course, if Isabella is speaking to one of her friends, she says, 'Ça va?' and the friend replies, '**Ça va, merci, et toi?**'"

"You mean, they use the same words for 'How are you?' and 'I'm alright'?" asked Sir Ralph, frowning.

"That's correct, sir," said Max. "'Ça va?' is a friendlier way of saying, 'How are you?' and of course, when you reply, you use 'toi' if you know someone well and 'vous' if you know them less well."

"Well, I'm pleased we sorted that out, Max. I'd hate to call someone important 'a little cabbage' by mistake!"

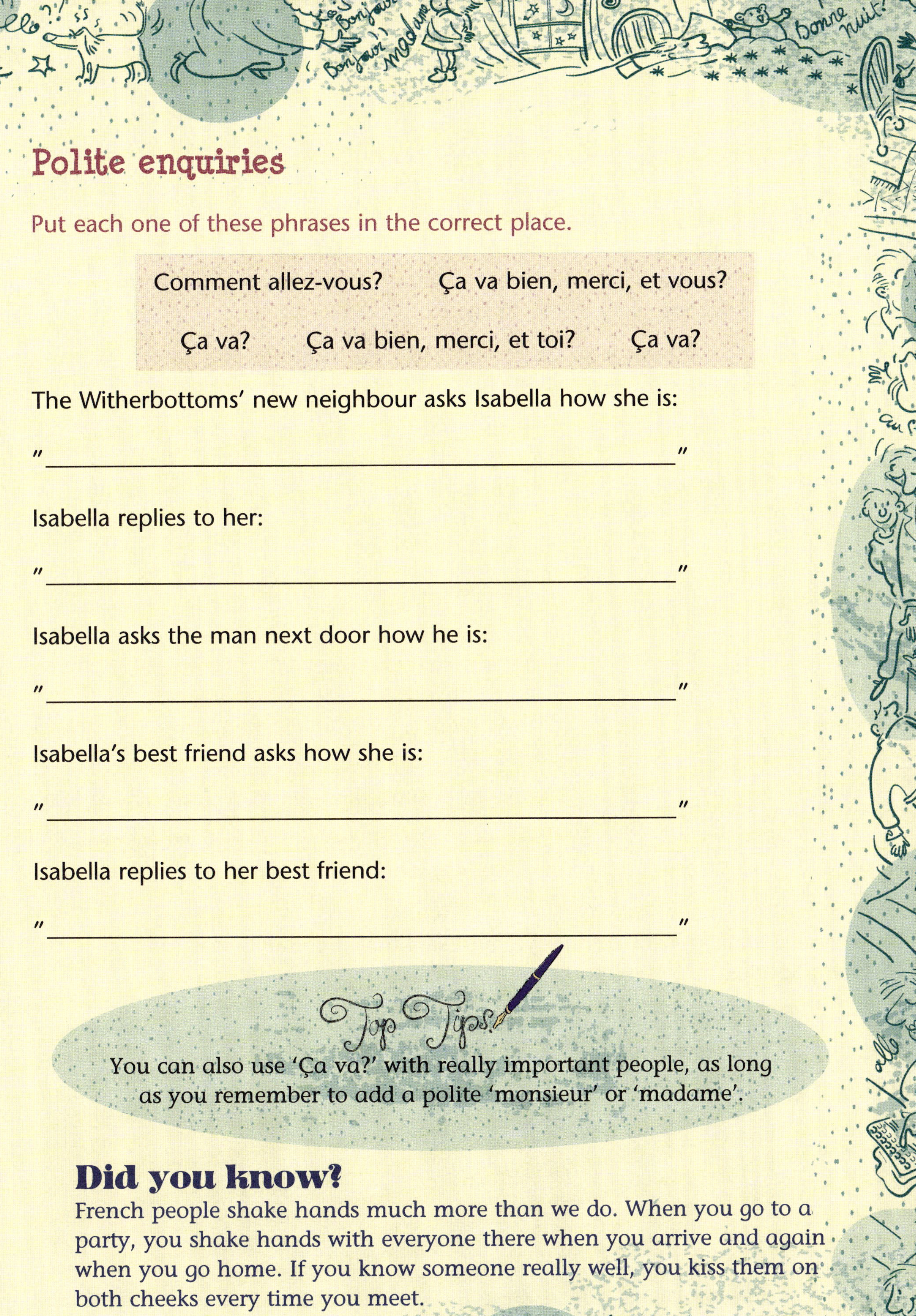

Polite enquiries

Put each one of these phrases in the correct place.

Comment allez-vous? Ça va bien, merci, et vous?

Ça va? Ça va bien, merci, et toi? Ça va?

The Witherbottoms' new neighbour asks Isabella how she is:

"____"

Isabella replies to her:

"____"

Isabella asks the man next door how he is:

"____"

Isabella's best friend asks how she is:

"____"

Isabella replies to her best friend:

"____"

Top Tips!

You can also use 'Ça va?' with really important people, as long as you remember to add a polite 'monsieur' or 'madame'.

Did you know?

French people shake hands much more than we do. When you go to a party, you shake hands with everyone there when you arrive and again when you go home. If you know someone really well, you kiss them on both cheeks every time you meet.

Knock, knock. Who's there?

Toc, Tock. Qui est là?

One morning, Mademoiselle Isabella Witherbottom was woken early by someone knocking very loudly at the front door.

"Goodness, I wonder who that could be?" she thought. She hadn't had a chance to wake up properly yet.

Bleary-eyed, she stumbled down the stairs, opened the door and made out the hazy image of a tall man with a dog by his side. She remembered her manners and said, "**Bonjour**."

"Bonjour," replied the man.

"**Comment vous appelez-vous?**" said Isabella to the man. "**Comment t'appelles-tu?**" she said to the dog. "**Je m'appelle** Isabella Witherbottom," she added, to introduce herself to the visitors.

There was a silence and the man cleared his throat.

"**C'est moi** – Max!" he said. "Sorry, I forgot my front door key when Spotless and I went for our morning walk!"

Isabella blinked, rubbed her eyes and saw that it certainly was Max and Spotless!

Who has come to visit?

A visitor has come to see the Witherbottoms, but who is it? Fill in the missing word in each sentence to work out who the visitor is. The first one has been done for you.

Max hears the door bell, so opens the front door.

"Comment ______ t'appelles-tu?" Max asks the little boy standing on the doorstep.

An aeroplane is flying overhead, so the boy does not hear Max properly.

"Comment ______-tu?" asks Max again, as a delivery van brakes noisily on the gravel drive.

He repeats the question.

"Comment t'appelles-______?" The little boy understands at last.

"Je ______ Alexandre," he replies, but now Max can't hear properly, as Spotless starts to bark.

"Je m'appelle ______ !" shouts the little boy.

Suddenly, Max realises what the boy has said.

Who has come to visit? ______

Top Tips!

When you are talking to adults or more than one person, you use 'Comment vous appelez-vous?'. When you are talking to other children or animals you use 'Comment t'appelles-tu?'.

Did you know?

'Je m'appelle' really means, 'I call myself' and the question asked is 'what do you call yourself?'. There are often differences in the way words are put together in different languages. If you can work out what people are actually saying, it makes it much easier to remember.

Revise Time

1 How do you say the following in French? Put a circle round the correct word.

a Hello — salut bonjour au revoir

b Good day — bonne nuit bonjour allô

c Good night — bonsoir bonjour bonne nuit

d See you soon — à bientôt au revoir salut

e Goodbye — salut au revoir bonjour

2 Which words or phrases should they use? Fill in the correct greetings.

a Max answers the phone.

____

b Sir Ralph wishes the old lady next door a good morning.

____

c Isabella goes to bed. What does she say to Sir Ralph's guests?

____

d Isabella says, 'Hello' to a friend she bumps into at the market.

____

3 Put these words in the right order to form sentences asking someone how they are and then replying.

a allez-vous Comment? ________________________

b merci vous et bien Très? ________________________

c va Ça? ________________________

d toi merci va Ça et? ________________________

e mon chou petit va Ça? ________________________

4 **Use these words to make five phrases asking how people are and replying when they ask you. Write out the five phrases.**

Comment va. Ça allez- toi? et merci Ça et vous? Ça merci vous? va? va Ça va

a ______________________

b ______________________

c ______________________

d ______________________

e ______________________

5 **'Comment vous appelez-vous?' and 'Comment t'appelles-tu?' mean, 'What is your name?'. In which of these situations would it be best to use, 'Comment t'appelles-tu?' Put a tick by them.**

a Max, when he is talking to one of Isabella's friends. ☐

b Sir Ralph, when he is asking a new customer his name. ☐

c Isabella, when she meets a young girl at a party. ☐

d Max, when he takes a message on the phone for Sir Ralph. ☐

e The receptionist, when Isabella goes to the dentist. ☐

6 **Rearrange these sentences to make a conversation.**

Je m'appelle Isabella. ______________________

Je m'appelle Madame Dupont. ______________________

Bonjour. ______________________

Comment vous appelez-vous? ______________________

Ten green bottles
Dix bouteilles vertes

Sir Ralph was in a pickle. Yesterday he made some of his special medicines for his new French neighbours. When he had finished, he carefully numbered each of the bottles and his laboratory assistant used a cassette player to record what each numbered bottle contained.

It was a very windy night, however, and as the windows were rather drafty, the labels had all been blown off. When Sir Ralph came into the lab this morning, the labels were all over the floor.

8
huit

So what's the number eight got to do with fields of wheat?!

Sir Ralph knew he could use the laboratory assistant's recorded notes, but they were in French and Sir Ralph was having trouble remembering his French numbers.

Max came to the rescue and wrote him a list of the numbers 1 to 10 in French and how they sounded. Then Sir Ralph sat scratching his head, looking at the list and listening to the cassette recorder, trying to work out which number should go on each bottle!

Number	How to write it	How to say it
1	un	urn
2	deux	der
3	trois	twa
4	quatre	catre
5	cinq	sank
6	six	seess
7	sept	set
8	huit	wheat
9	neuf	nerf
10	dix	dees

What is in the mystery bottle?

Match the numbers on the labels with the names of the potions. Then write the first letter of each name on the correct bottle labels. The first one has been done for you.

Can you read what French words the bottles spell when in a line 1 to 10? It is Isabella's favourite treat!

dix	Eau d'été	**un**	Lessive d'estomac
six	Orange amère	**deux**	Âme de désert
quatre	Isolation de lait	**huit**	Alimentation de nuit
sept	Noisette noire	**cinq**	Merveille de coeur
trois	Lait de montagne	**neuf**	Don des anges

It will help you to learn your numbers if you read them out loud a few times. Then see how many you can do without looking.

Did you know?

In France, they write the number 1 with quite a big tail on the top. They also put a little bar across the number 7, so that 1s and 7s do not get confused. If you saw a French person write these numbers, they would look like this:

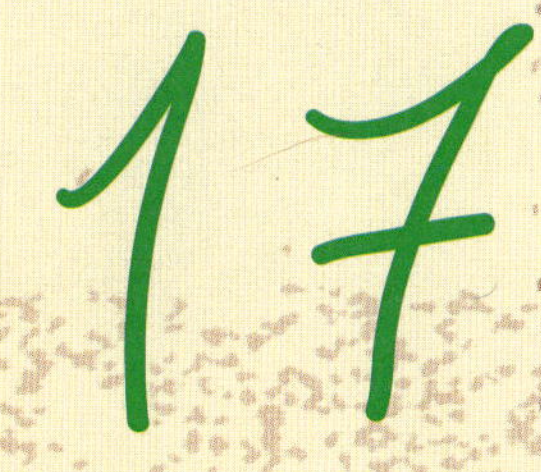

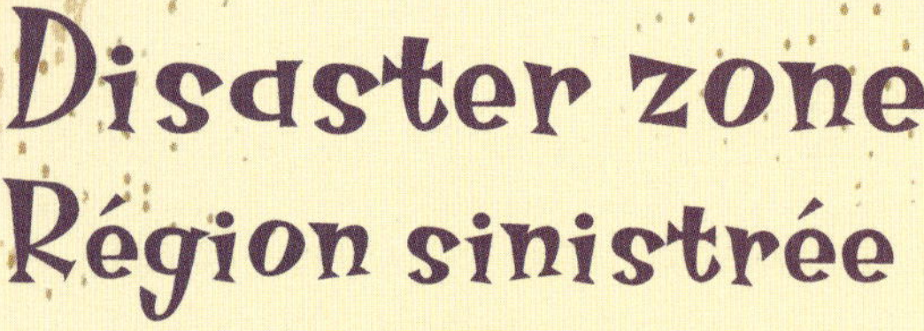

Disaster zone
Région sinistrée

Isabella was going to visit the Marché aux Puces, a big flea market. Her bedroom was a mess, so she could not find anything she needed. The housekeeper might be able to find them, but she did not speak English. Max helped Isabella to make a list in French.

"I'll need my pen," she said to Max, "so I can make a list of all the things I'd like to buy."

Max wrote, "Où est mon **stylo**?"

"Oh, and my ruler for measuring the picture frames I want to buy." Max added to the list, "Où est ma **règle**?"

"Also, I'll take my sketch pad, my pencil and my felt tips, because I'm sure I'll find some good things to sketch there. I'll also need my rubber."

Max wrote down, "Où sont mon **carnet de croquis**, mon **crayon**, mes **feutres** et ma **gomme**?"

"I'll take my calculator as well, so I can check how much I'm spending."

"Et ma **calculette**," wrote Max.

"I'll need my folder to put my sketches in," said Isabella.

Max muttered as he wrote, "Et mon **classeur**?"

Isabella looked at the list. "That's the lot, I think," she said. "Bon!"

"Let's hope the housekeeper can find all these things in your bedroom, which looks more like a disaster zone!" said Max, as he took the list and went in search of the housekeeper.

Stylo, règle, feutres, calculette, crayon, gomme, classeur? No, nothing but bones here, I'm afraid.

Help Isabella to find her belongings

Find all Isabella's missing objects in the wordsearch.

c	a	r	n	e	t	t	r	a	b	è	d
l	a	f	g	d	e	j	k	l	m	n	o
a	e	l	r	s	c	r	o	q	u	i	s
s	t	o	v	a	n	n	p	t	d	c	c
s	t	h	l	u	o	g	n	e	g	f	f
e	e	o	h	y	l	j	j	k	o	l	i
u	l	m	a	o	t	a	q	r	m	t	u
r	u	r	t	u	v	s	v	y	m	o	u
v	c	w	x	f	e	u	t	r	e	s	o
w	l	o	q	u	i	s	a	b	i	b	c
w	a	b	y	c	n	d	è	e	e	c	m
f	c	g	h	h	h	i	e	l	g	è	r

Top Tips!

'Mon' is the **masculine** word for 'my' and is also used for **feminine** words that begin with a vowel or a silent 'h'. 'Ma' is used for all other feminine words and 'mes' is used for all plurals.

Did you know?

French exercise books all have squares rather than just lines on them. You can see them in French supermarkets during the summer holidays, because French children have to provide their own writing materials for school. They often come in lots of colourful varieties.

Donkey's years
L'âge de l'âne

Sir Ralph Witherbottom and Isabella were going to help one of the neighbours with a birthday party. Isabella had volunteered to put together all the goody-bags for the children to take home. Sir Ralph and Max were helping her.

"It's really a good idea to label each one to show whether it's for a boy or a girl and for what age," said Max. "Look at the one I've done."

Sir Ralph read the label, "**Pour un garçon de sept ans**." Sir Ralph frowned.

"Why does she need to know how many donkeys they have?" asked Sir Ralph.

It was Max's turn to frown. "You're thinking of '**âne**', the French word for 'donkey'. The word for 'year' is 'an'," said Max, trying not to smirk.

"Oh, I see," Sir Ralph laughed. "So not seven donkeys, but seven years old!"

"How do we write 'for a girl of eight'?"

"Pour **une fille** de **huit** ans," replied Max.

"What should I say to find out how old they are?" asked Isabella.

"You should say, '**Quel âge as-tu?**' and they'll reply with something like, '**J'ai** sept ans'," explained Max.

He and Isabella then started to help Max to write some more labels.

Whose goody-bag?

Isabella asked the children 'Quel âge as-tu?' and this is how they replied.

Pierre said, "J'ai neuf ans."
Marc said, "J'ai dix ans."
Chantal said, "J'ai quatre ans."

Marie said, "J'ai six ans."
Antoine said, "J'ai cinq ans."
Annette said, "J'ai sept ans."

Now link the goody-bags to the names.

pour un garçon de 5 ans

pour un garçon de 10 ans

pour un garçon de 9 ans

Pierre

Marie

Marc

Antoine

Chantal

Annette

pour une fille de 6 ans

pour une fille de 4 ans

pour une fille de 7 ans

Top Tips!

'J'ai sept ans' really means 'I have seven years'. 'Quel âge as-tu?' really means 'which age do you have?'. French people 'have' an age rather than 'are' an age.

Did you know?

Old people in France belong to the 'troisième âge' – the third age. The first is your time at school. The second is where you work and support a family perhaps. The third is after you retire. People about the age of your parents are often referred to as being 'd'un certain âge' – of a certain age.

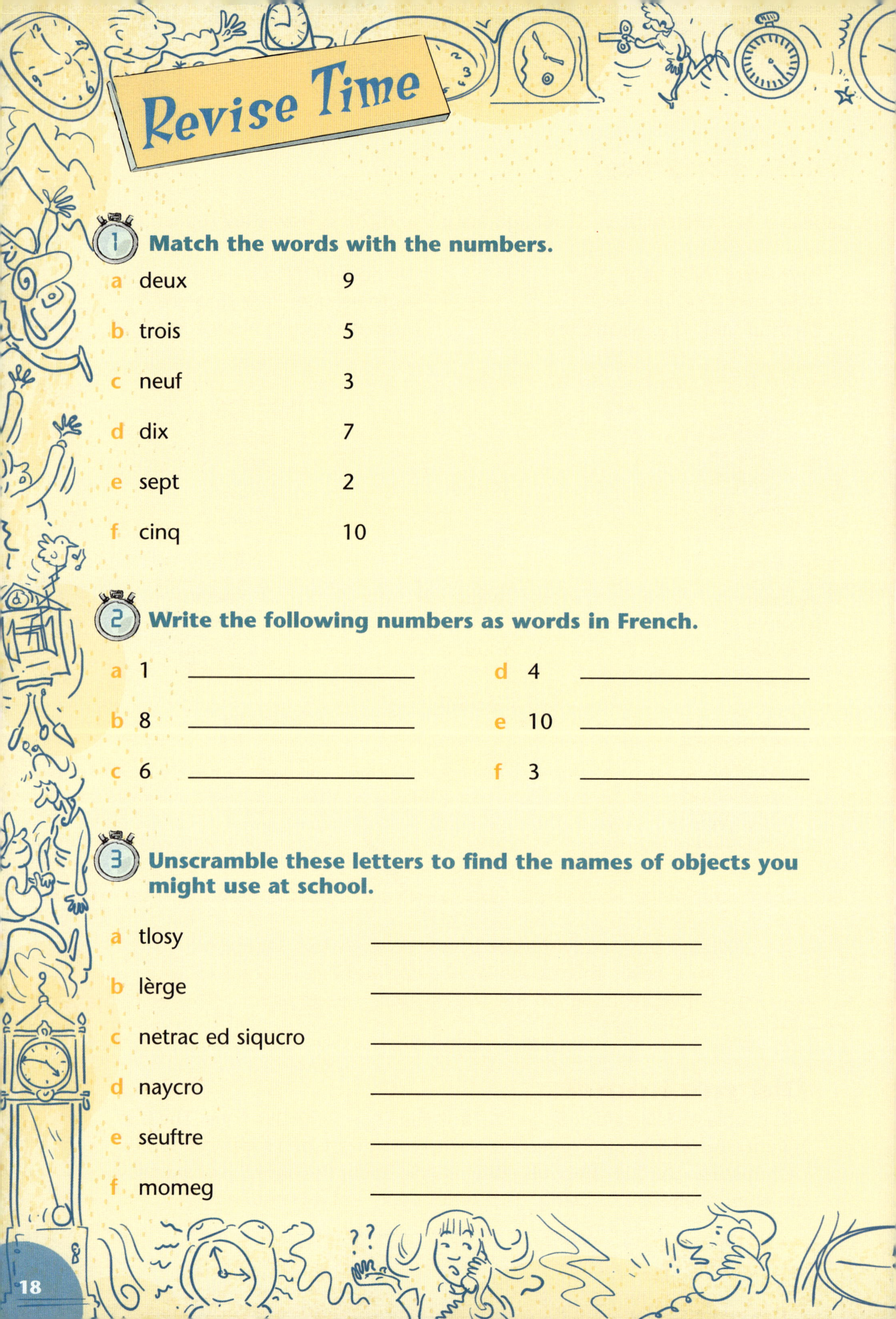

Revise Time

1 Match the words with the numbers.

a deux 9

b trois 5

c neuf 3

d dix 7

e sept 2

f cinq 10

2 Write the following numbers as words in French.

a 1 ______________________

b 8 ______________________

c 6 ______________________

d 4 ______________________

e 10 ______________________

f 3 ______________________

3 Unscramble these letters to find the names of objects you might use at school.

a tlosy ______________________

b lèrge ______________________

c netrac ed siqucro ______________________

d naycro ______________________

e seuftre ______________________

f momeg ______________________

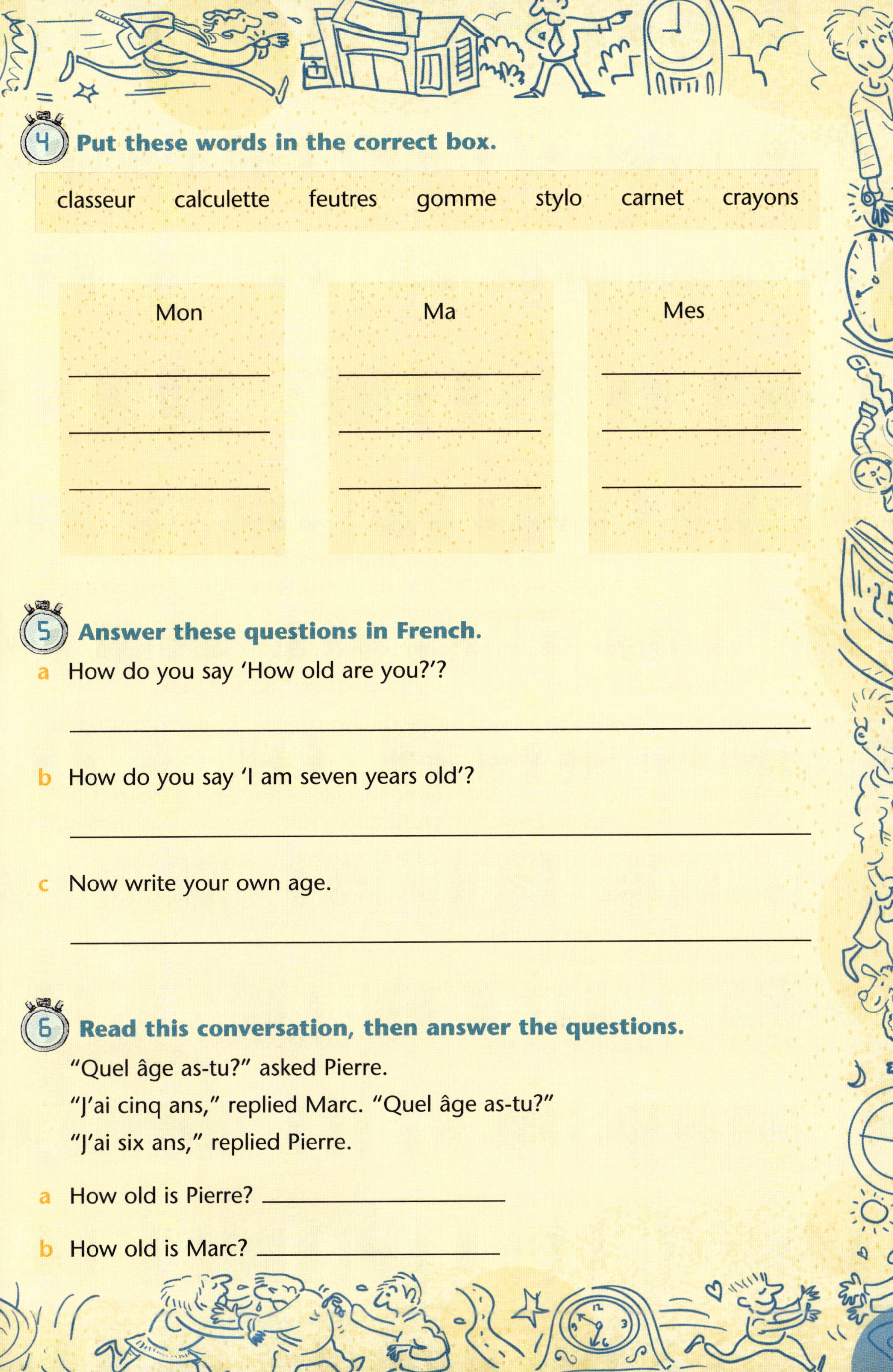

4 Put these words in the correct box.

classeur calculette feutres gomme stylo carnet crayons

Mon	Ma	Mes
____________	____________	____________
____________	____________	____________
____________	____________	____________

5 Answer these questions in French.

a How do you say 'How old are you?'?

____

b How do you say 'I am seven years old'?

____

c Now write your own age.

____

6 Read this conversation, then answer the questions.

"Quel âge as-tu?" asked Pierre.

"J'ai cinq ans," replied Marc. "Quel âge as-tu?"

"J'ai six ans," replied Pierre.

a How old is Pierre? ____________

b How old is Marc? ____________

At home with the Witherbottoms
Chez les Witherbottom

Sir Ralph wants some furniture for their new house. He is telling Max what is needed, whilst Max is speaking on the phone to the furniture shop.

"We need two armchairs and a settee for the living room," said Sir Ralph.

"Nous avons besoin de deux **fauteuils** et d'un **canapé** pour le **salon**," said Max.

"Izzy needs a new bed," continued Sir Ralph. "I need a wardrobe and a chest of drawers."

"Aussi, un **lit** pour la **chambre** de Mademoiselle," explained Max to the shop assistant. "Une **armoire** et une **commode** pour Monsieur."

"We need three chairs and a table in the kitchen," said Sir Ralph.

"Trois **chaises** et une **table** pour la **cuisine**," added Max.

"We really must have a lamp in the dining room," Sir Ralph muttered.

"Une **lampe** pour la **salle à manger**?" Max asked.

"Yes and we also need another set of shelves in the dining room." Sir Ralph scratched his head, which he often did when he was thinking!

"Et une **étagère** en plus pour la salle à manger," continued Max.

There was a pause.

"Non, rien pour la **cave** ou la **salle de bains**," answered Max finally.

"What was all that about?" asked Sir Ralph, after Max had put the phone down.

"He asked whether we wanted anything for the cellar or the bathroom."

"Thankfully we have a bath at least!" laughed Sir Ralph.

Where shall I put it?

Link up the phrases to show what furniture Sir Ralph wants for which rooms. Some rooms will have more than one item in them.

les deux fauteuils	dans la chambre de Monsieur
la table	dans la chambre de Mademoiselle
les trois chaises	dans le salon
la lampe	dans la cuisine
le lit	dans la salle à manger
la commode	
l'armoire	
l'étagère	

Top Tips!

Usually French words ending in 'e' are feminine. You can see this in the words for furniture and rooms. The 'é' in 'canapé' does not count because of the accent.

Did you know?

French lounge-dining rooms are often furnished a little differently from ours. In smaller homes, the dining table and chairs will be right in the middle of the room, taking up most of the space, with the armchairs, sofa and television round the edge. French families love to spend a long time at the table, eating their meals and chatting afterwards.

France

Grande-Bretagne

Italie

Mind your language!
Sois Poli!

Sir Ralph wanted to send a letter about his latest invention to people all around the world. He was looking at a French atlas.

"I see," he said. "'**Belgique**' is Belgium, '**Espagne**' is Spain, '**Italie**' is Italy, '**Irlande**' is Ireland and '**Grèce**' is Greece. They're easy. '**Luxembourg**', '**Portugal**' and '**France**' are obvious. What about these others, though?"

"'**Allemagne**' is Germany, sir," said Max. "'**Angleterre**' is England, '**Écosse**' is Scotland, '**Pays Bas**' is The Netherlands, '**Pays de Galles**' is Wales and '**Suisse**' is Switzerland."

Max was looking at a book which told him about which languages were spoken in different countries. He made a few notes to work out which would be the best language to use to write the letter being sent to each country.

"We'll have to use '**allemand**', German, for Germany and it's also one of the languages spoken in Switzerland," he said to Sir Ralph. '**Anglais**' is English and they speak English in Wales, Scotland and Ireland too. The Dutch can also speak it quite well, although they have their own language, '**néerlandais**'. In Belgium, one third of the people speak '**français**', French, which is also spoken in Luxemburg, Switzerland and, of course, France. The rest of the Belgians speak '**flamand**', Flemish, which is very similar to Dutch. They speak '**italien**' in Italy and Switzerland. Then there's '**grec**' for Greece, '**espagnol**' for Spain, and '**portugais**' for Portugal. Luxemburg also has '**luxembourgeois**'. '**Gallois**' is also spoken in Wales and '**irlandais**' is also spoken in Ireland."

"Gosh, we're going to need some help translating my letter into all these languages," said Sir Ralph. "This is much harder than my daily newspaper crossword!"

Letters and envelopes

Link up these letters written in different languages with the correct envelope.

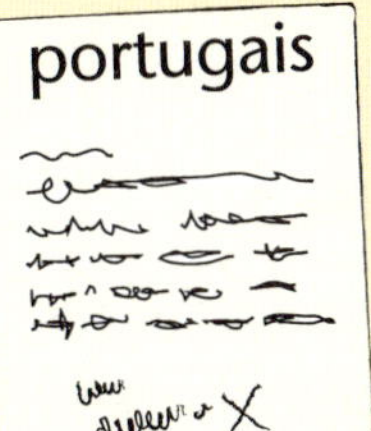

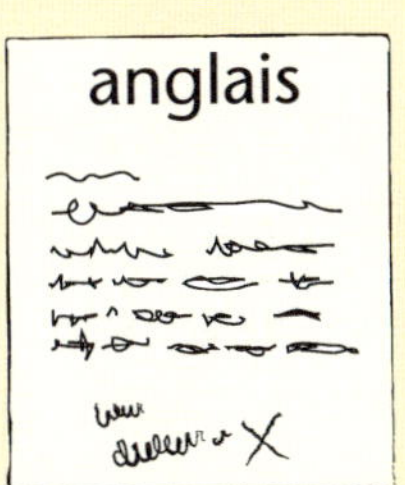

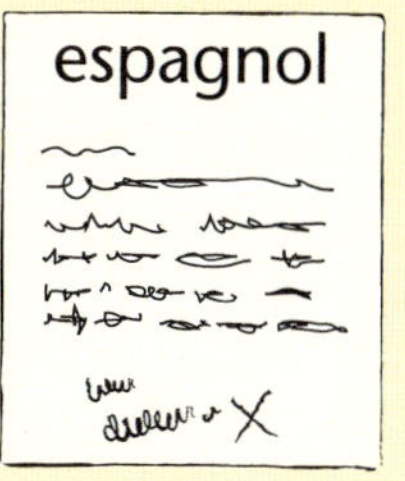

You use '**en**' for 'in' or 'to' a feminine country. You use '**au**' with masculine countries, so it's 'au Luxembourg' and 'au Portugal'. The Netherlands is masculine plural, so it's 'aux Pays Bas'.

Did you know?

French is the official language of 21 countries. It is an important language in several others, including parts of Africa and the island of Jersey. 6,250,000 people in Canada and 2,400,000 in the United States use it as their first language. Diplomats also often use it as an international language.

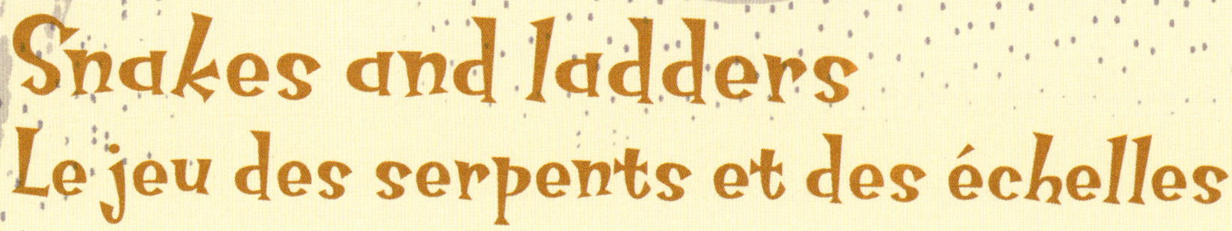

Snakes and ladders
Le jeu des serpents et des échelles

Isabella was using a new 'Snakes and Ladders' computer programme. All of the instructions were in French. She clicked on the picture of a dice. It jiggled around and then turned to six.

"**Case numéro six**," called the computer. "**Encore un tour**." Her counter moved to square number six.

Isabella clicked on the dice again. She had another six!

"Sept, huit, neuf, dix, **onze**, **douze**," called the computer. "Encore un tour."

Isabella's next turn showed a five.

"**Treize**, **quatorze**, **quinze**, **seize**, **dix-sept**," said the computer. Isabella's counter moved to number seventeen.

It was the computer's turn and it managed three sixes in a row. "**Dix-huit**!" it called as it moved to eighteen. "**Une échelle**."

Isabella watched in dismay as the computer's counter climbed up the ladder to number twenty-seven. "**Vingt-sept**," called the computer.

The next dice showed three. The counter moved to number thirty. "**Vingt-huit**, **vingt-neuf**, **trente**," counted the computer.

Isabella's next dice turned to five.

"**Dix-huit**, **dix-neuf**, **vingt**, **vingt et un**, **vingt-deux**," said the computer. Isabella's counter moved to twenty-two.

Isabella sniggered when the computer's counter moved to thirty-one, where there was a nice fat snake.

"**Trente et un**. **Un serpent**," said the computer. Its counter slid down to square number fourteen.

Isabella's next go was a four.

"**Vingt-trois**, **vingt-quatre**, **vingt-cinq**, **vingt-six**," counted the computer.

"Non! Encore un serpent!" cried Isabella, before the computer could deliver the bad news!

Time to play

Play computer snakes and ladders. Draw the route you would follow if you threw the dice numbers shown and follow the instructions.

Your dice throws:	**The computer's instructions:**
"Trois"	"Un, deux, trois. Case numéro trois. Une échelle."
"Cinq"	"Huit, neuf, dix, onze, douze. Case numéro douze."
"Six"	"Treize, quatorze, quinze, seize, dix-sept, dix-huit. Case numéro dix-huit. Une échelle. Encore un tour."
"Quatre"	"Vingt-huit, vingt-neuf, trente, trente et un. Case numéro trente et un. Un serpent."
"Un"	"Quinze. Case numéro quinze."
"Trois"	"Seize. Dix-sept, dix-huit. "

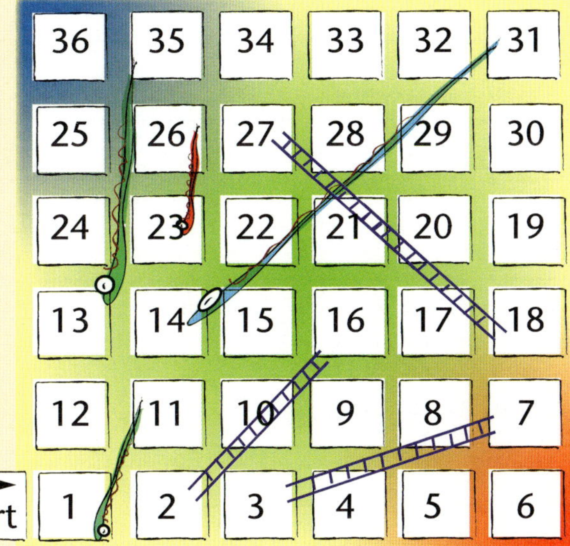

Where are you now? ______________

Top Tips

Be careful with numbers ending in 'one'. Twenty-one is 'vingt *et* un' and thirty-one is 'trente *et* un'. You are really saying 'twenty *and* one' and 'thirty *and* one.'

Did you know?

Bigger numbers in French and in English are made up of smaller ones. Numbers 1–19 in English and 1–16 in French have their own names. The others are made by combining numbers. 'Dix-sept', 'dix-huit' and 'dix-neuf' are each made up of 'ten' and another number. You can see how numbers are used together even more clearly in 'vingt-deux' and 'twenty-two'.

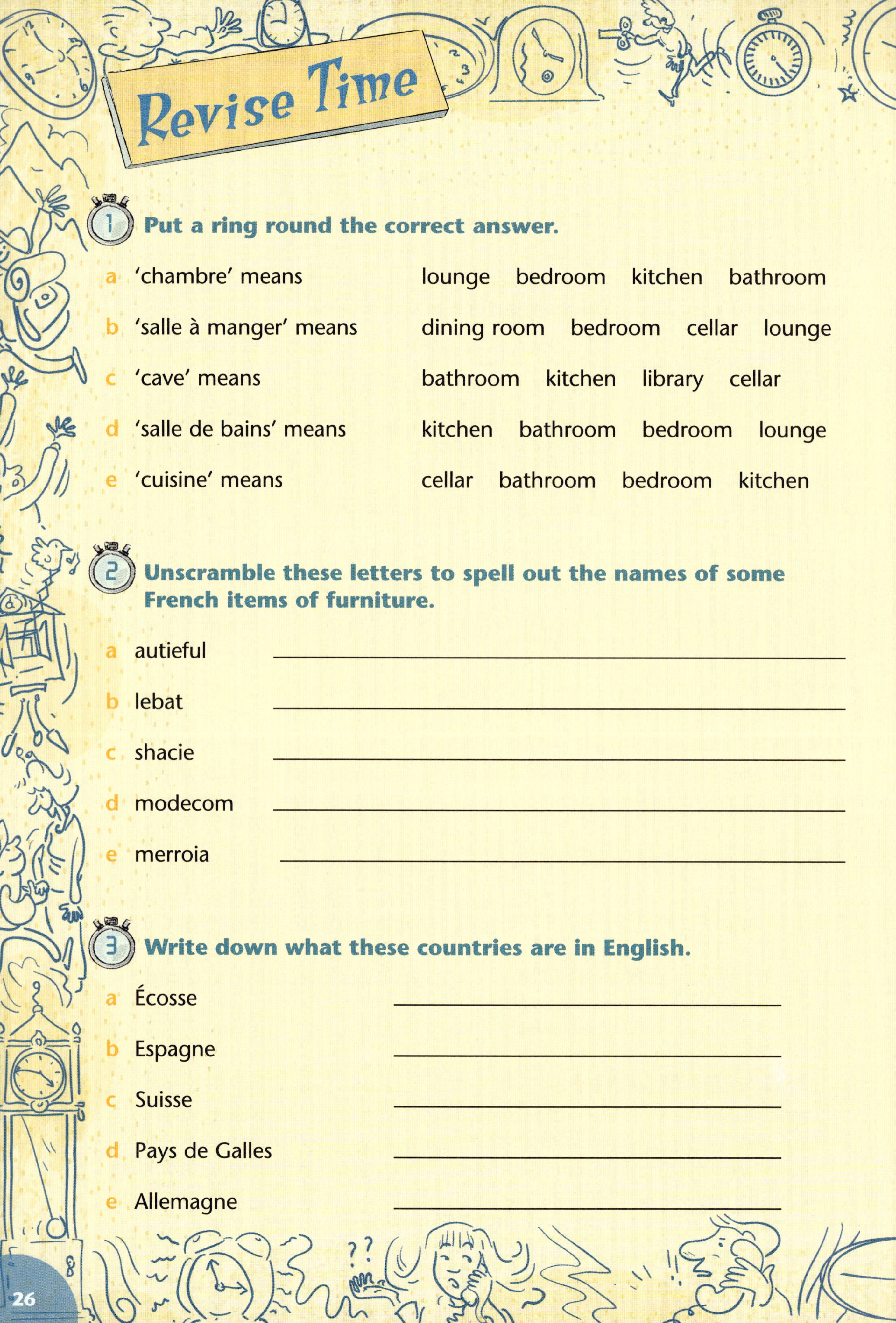

Revise Time

1 Put a ring round the correct answer.

a 'chambre' means — lounge bedroom kitchen bathroom

b 'salle à manger' means — dining room bedroom cellar lounge

c 'cave' means — bathroom kitchen library cellar

d 'salle de bains' means — kitchen bathroom bedroom lounge

e 'cuisine' means — cellar bathroom bedroom kitchen

2 Unscramble these letters to spell out the names of some French items of furniture.

a autieful ____________________

b lebat ____________________

c shacie ____________________

d modecom ____________________

e merroia ____________________

3 Write down what these countries are in English.

a Écosse ____________________

b Espagne ____________________

c Suisse ____________________

d Pays de Galles ____________________

e Allemagne ____________________

4 **'Vrai' means true and 'faux' means false. Write 'vrai' or 'faux' next to each of these statements.**

a En France on parle français. ______________

b En Allemagne on parle allemand. ______________

c En Suisse on parle espagnol. ______________

d En Écosse on parle gallois. ______________

e Au Portugal on parle italien. ______________

5 **Underline the word that matches the figure.**

a 11 onze douze quatorze seize

b 14 treize quatorze quinze dix-sept

c 20 dix-huit vingt vingt-trois trente

d 26 seize vingt-cinq vingt-six trente

e 31 treize vingt-trois trente trente et un

6 **Write down the next number in these lists of words.**

a huit neuf dix ______________

b douze treize quatorze ______________

c seize dix-sept dix-huit ______________

d vingt vingt et un vingt-deux ______________

e vingt-quatre vingt-cinq vingt-six ______________

f vingt-huit vingt-neuf trente ______________

Stormy weather overhead!
Des orages dans le ciel!

Max and Sir Ralph were watching the weather forecast on the television in the attic office. The wind was lashing at the windows and the rain was thundering on the roof.

The presenter started off by saying, "**Il fait mauvais presque partout**."

"Well, it seems we're not the only ones having bad weather," said Max.

The presenter pointed to their town on the map. "**Il y a des orages**," she said.

"She's right," said Max. "We certainly are having storms."

"Il fait **chaud**," she said, pointing to a thermometer showing 24 degrees in the south.

"Maybe we should go on a trip to the beach. At least it's hot there," said Sir Ralph.

Next, the presenter pointed to the mountains and said, "Il **neige**."

"Or maybe we could go skiing," suggested Max. "Looks like there's some good snow up in the Alps."

"Il fait **froid**," she added, pointing to a thermometer showing – 6 degrees.

"That is cold! I think I like the beach trip idea a lot better!" said Sir Ralph.

Pouf! Il fait chaud. Too hot to be wearing a fur coat!

"Il y a **du vent**," she said, pointing to the symbol for wind in the west. She then turned to the east. "Il y a **du brouillard**," she added. There was a symbol for fog.

"Demain, il fera **beau** partout." She smiled and continued. "Il y aura du **soleil**." She showed a picture of the sun.

"Well, if it's going to be nice tomorrow, maybe we'll just stay right here after all," said Max. He went to look out of the window at the pouring rain.

"Il **pleut à verse**," he said. "That's how you say 'it's pouring'."

"Maybe we should turn up the heating just for today, anyway," sighed Sir Ralph.

La météo

Draw weather symbols on the map to match the written labels.

Top Tips!

You use 'il y a' and 'il fait' for weather that is happening now, and 'il y aura' and 'il fera' for weather which is going to happen later on.

Did you know?

The weather really can vary greatly from one part of France to another. For example, in April it is quite possible for people to be skiing in the mountains while others are sunbathing on the south coast.

A fine mess!

Un beau désordre!

"I'll never get this sorted out," said Isabella. "It'll be a real mess if I don't spell everyone's name right."

She had volunteered to sell tickets for the play at La Maison des Jeunes, the Youth Centre, the following week. People kept phoning and she had to ask them how to spell their names and then write them down. She kept getting muddled with her French alphabet.

"Right," said Max. "I'll say the letters out loud and you write down the way they sound. 'Ah', 'bay', 'say', 'day'," he started.

Isabella wrote down A, B, C, D... and underneath the letters she wrote how they sounded, until they had finished the whole alphabet.

Here are Isabella's notes:

A	B	C	D	E
ah	bay	say	day	euh
F	G	H	I	J
eff	jay	ash	ee	jee
K	L	M	N	O
kah	ell	emm	enn	oh
P	Q	R	S	T
pay	coo	air	ess	tay
U	V	W		X
oo	vay	dooblavay		icks
Y		Z		
ee greck		zed		

"There," said Max, as she finished. "Now you shouldn't make any mistakes with people's names."

What is the name?

Say the letter sounds out loud. Then write in the letters to spell people's names.

1 pay ee euh air air euh — — — — — —

day oo pay oh enn tay — — — — — —

2 ah enn tay oh ee enn euh — — — — — — —

ell euh say ell euh air say — — — — — — —

3 emm ah air ee euh — — — — —

jee ah emm euh ell ell euh — — — — — — —

4 ess oo zed ah enn enn euh — — — — — — —

day euh jay ah oo ell ell euh — — — — — — — —

5 emm ah air say — — — —

day oo vay ah ell — — — — —

6 jee euh ah enn enn euh — — — — — —

ell euh jay air ah enn day — — — — — — —

Top Tips!

French 'g' is pronounced 'jay', like our 'j', and 'j' is pronounced 'jee', almost like our 'g'. They are the other way round!

Did you know?

You do not have to worry about pronouncing the 'h' at the beginning of a word in French. It is silent. Most words beginning with 'h' are treated as words beginning with a **vowel**, so for example **le** or **la** become shortened to **l'**. There are some exceptions, like Le Havre – a town in France.

A strange family
Une famille bizarre

Isabella was reading a book. She was able to read French quite well now, but she was finding it difficult to understand the strange family connections in the story. Fortunately, at the back of the book was a family tree showing exactly how everyone was related, which she was showing to Max.

"'Madame Marie Flétrifond est la **mère** d'Alexandre Flétrifond'," she read out to Max. "So Mrs Flétrifond is the mother and Alexandre is the son. Oh yes, and of course, there's his father. 'Son **père** s'appelle Monsieur Alain Flétrifond'."

"'Le **frère** d'Alexandre s'appelle Martin et sa **soeur** s'appelle Marianne'," she carried on reading. "So, Alexandre's brother is called Martin and his sister is called Marianne."

"'Le **grand-père** d'Alexandre s'appelle Monsieur Pomme de Terre et la **grand-mère** s'appelle Madame Pomme de Terre'," Isabella continued. "So that's grandfather and grandmother, Mr and Mrs Potato?"

"'**L'oncle** d'Alexandre s'appelle Marc Renault'." She giggled. "His uncle sounds more like a car than a person."

Bonjour grand-mère Carotte! Ça va?

She carried on reading. "'Sa **tante** s'appelle Annette Renault. Il a aussi un **cousin** Pierre et une **cousine** Yvette.' Oh, I see," she said. "You add an 'e' on for 'girl cousin', otherwise it's the same word as in English."

"Goodness," said Isabella, "I'm glad my family isn't as strange as this one!"

"Actually," said Max, looking at the book, "'flétri' means 'wither' and 'fond' means 'bottom', as in the bottom of a well or pudding basin, so the 'flétrifonds' in this book are actually the ...Witherbottoms!"

alphabet A B C D E F G H I J K L M N

Who am I?

Use the family tree opposite to help you work out who these people are.

1 Ma mère s'appelle Annette Renault. Ma soeur s'appelle Yvette.

____

2 Mon frère s'appelle Alexandre. Ma soeur s'appelle Marianne.

____

3 Mon père s'appelle Alain. Mes frères s'appellent Martin et Alexandre.

____

4 Ma mère s'appelle Madame Pomme de Terre. Ma soeur s'appelle Marie.

____

5 Mon grand-père s'appelle Monsieur Pomme de Terre. Mon frère s'appelle Pierre.

____

Top Tips!

There are three words for 'his' in French - 'son' for **masculine**, 'sa' for **feminine** and '**ses**' for plural. Surprisingly, 'son', 'sa' and 'ses' also mean 'her', because it is the word that follows it that makes it change not the owner.

Did you know?

The French for 'stepfather' or father-in-law is 'beau-père', which really means 'handsome father' or 'fine father'. 'Mother-in-law' and 'stepmother' are 'beautiful mother' or 'lovely mother' – 'belle-mère'. The words 'beau-frère' and 'belle-soeur' also mean brother-in-law and sister-in-law. So in the French version of the story, Cinderella had a lovely stepmother!

Revise Time

1 Here are some English phrases about the weather. Put a ring round the French phrase that means the same.

a It is nice. Il fait mauvais. Il fait froid. Il fait beau.

b It is sunny. Il y a du vent. Il y a du soleil. Il y a du brouillard.

c It is raining. Il pleut. Il neige. Il pleut à verse.

d It will be windy. Il y aura du brouillard. Il y a du vent. Il y aura du vent.

e It will be hot. Il fera chaud. Il fait chaud. Il fera froid.

2 What are these expressions telling us? Write them on the correct line

Il fait du vent. Il fera beau. Il y aura du brouillard. Il fait chaud.

a It is hot. ______________________

b It will be fine. ______________________

c It is windy. ______________________

d It will be foggy. ______________________

3 Write down the names that these French letter sounds spell.

a ee ess ah bay euh ell ell ah ______________________

b ess pay oh tay ell euh ess ess ______________________

c emm ah icks ______________________

d ess ee air air ah ell pay ash ______________________

4 Fill in the sound of the missing letter, then write out the sounds as letters.

a ah bay ____________ day euh _ _ _ _ _

b oo vay dooblavay icks ____________ zed _ _ _ _ _ _

c coo ____________ ess tay oo _ _ _ _ _

d eff jay ash ee ____________ _ _ _ _ _

e ____________ ell emm enn oh _ _ _ _ _

5 Work out which relations are hidden in this chain of letters. There are five altogether. The first letter of each word has been done for you.

o m p r e f è r r r e e è è d s g r a n e p u è r r - e

a m _ _ _

b p _ _ _

c f _ _ _ _

d s _ _ _ _

e g _ _ _ _ _ _ _ _ _

6 Write these sentences in French.

a My brother is called Simon. ______________________________

b My sister is called Annette. ______________________________

c His mother is called Mrs Dupont.

____

d Her cousin is called Paul. ______________________________

e My grandmother is called Mrs Laval.

____

Thanks a lot!
Merci bien!

"**Merci bien**," said Max, taking the letters from the postman. It was Sir Ralph's birthday and there were too many cards to go through the letterbox.

"**Je vous en prie**," replied the postman.

"That must mean 'think nothing of it'," thought Max.

Then a man came with a parcel for Sir Ralph. Isabella could only just carry it.

"Merci **beaucoup**," she said, from behind the large box.

"**Je t'en prie**," said the delivery man.

"He means 'think nothing of it'," thought Isabella.

Sir Ralph was very eager to have his next present. When he opened the door for the third time, he didn't read the paper the man was holding out to him and he didn't look too closely at the lorry parked in the drive.

"Merci, Monsieur, merci!" he cried.

"**De rien**," said the man, shrugging his shoulders as if to say, 'It's nothing'. Soon he was tipping manure all over the garden. Max had ordered it to help grow his newly planted seeds in the vegetable patch.

Isabella, Max and Spotless came running to the front door to see where the smell was coming from. It was so strong, it had wafted into the breakfast room. Sir Ralph didn't think this was much of a present!

Max was very happy though and started a letter to the firm which had supplied the manure.

"**Je vous remercie de** ..." He was so pleased that he had found the exact words for 'I thank you ...'.

Crossword

Use the clues to complete the crossword.

Verticalement
1 A lot
2 Very much
4 It's nothing

Horizontalement
3 Thank you
5 Sir

Top Tips!

After 'merci', 'je t'en prie' is for a friend, and 'je vous en prie' for several people or one person you do not know well. 'De rien' is for anyone.

Did you know?

'Merci' is also the French word for 'mercy'. A 'mercier' is a haberdasher, a person who sells little bits and pieces, such as buttons or safety-pins, not someone who has the task of thanking people!

Some dates for your diary
Des dates pour ton agenda

Isabella had got into a real muddle with her dates. She had almost missed her dentist's appointment, so Max bought her a brand new calendar to put up in the hallway. It had all of the months of the year in it. Max was helping her to pin it up on the wall.

"Oh yes, I see," she said. "It'll be easy to remember the months '**janvier**', '**février**', '**mars**'. They all begin with the same letter as in English – January, February, March."

"So do '**avril**', '**mai**' and '**juin**'," said Max.

"'Mai' sounds almost exactly the same as 'May'," said Isabella. "'**Juillet**' also begins with the same letter as July. '**Août**' – goodness, that does have a lot of **vowels** in it, but then so does August! '**Septembre**' is almost exactly the same, but the last two letters are swapped around."

"It's the same with '**octobre**', '**novembre**' and '**décembre**'," added Max.

Isabella started to fill in the calendar. Then she phoned a couple of people to confirm some dates.

The hairdresser said that her appointment was 'le premier juin', so Isabella wrote 'hairdresser' in the slot for the first of June.

Her friend Pierre told her that the boat trip was 'le seize mai'. She wrote 'boat trip' on the sixteenth of May and said, "I'm looking forward to that outing!"

Dates in the diary

Isabella spoke to some more people to be reminded about the dates of things she was doing in August, September and October. Join what the people said on the phone to the correct date with a line.

1 Louis said that the picnic in the woods was 'le vingt août'.

2 Simon said that the visit to the zoo was 'le vingt et un septembre'.

3 Suzanne announced that her birthday party would be 'le vingt-neuf septembre'.

4 The dentist's receptionist said the appointment was 'le vingt-sept octobre'.

5 Marie said that she was moving house 'le trente novembre'.

Août		
20	21	22
23	24	25
26	27	28
29	30	31

Octobre		
20	21	22
23	24	25
26	27	28
29	30	31

Top Tips!

There is no word for 'of' in French dates. You use the ordinary number, with the exception of 'premier', 'first', e.g., 'le deux février' and 'le premier mars'.

Did you know?

'Sept', 'septembre' and 'September' all come from the Latin word for 'seven' – 'septum'. Many French and English words come from Latin, which was spoken by the Romans. In one old Roman calendar, 'septembre' used to be the seventh month. 'Octobre' comes from the word for 'eight', 'novembre' from the word for 'nine' and 'décembre' from the word for 'ten'.

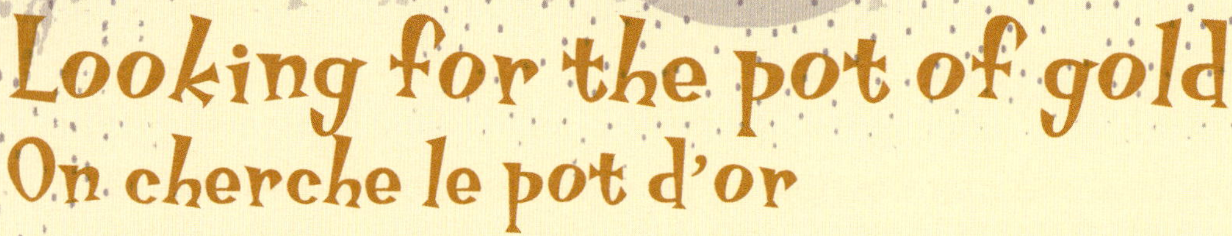

Looking for the pot of gold

On cherche le pot d'or

It had been raining all afternoon, but now the sun was coming out. Sir Ralph and Isabella were looking out of the window at a beautiful rainbow. "I wonder if there really is a pot of gold at the end," said Sir Ralph.

Isabella was not at all sure, but she loved all the colours! So, with Max's help, she wrote herself a list of all of the colours in the rainbow. Then she painted the rainbow and labelled it in French.

Un pot d'or? I'd rather have a big, juicy bone.

"It's easy, really, to remember these French colours," thought Isabella. "'**Rouge**' begins with the same letter as red. '**Orange**', '**violet**' and '**indigo**' are exactly the same in French and English. '**Bleu**' has got the same letters in it as blue, but the last two letters are swapped around. That just leaves '**jaune**' and '**vert**', which isn't too much to remember!"

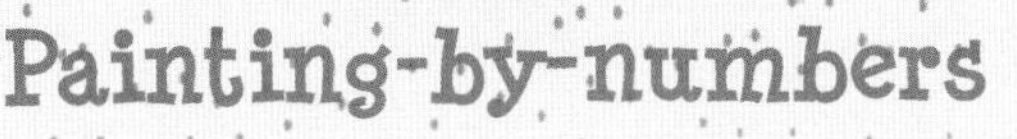

Painting-by-numbers

Isabella has a new painting-by-numbers kit. Use the key to colour the picture. Write the name of the monument below it.

Key

1 Rouge

2 Orange

3 Jaune

4 Vert

5 Bleu

6 Indigo

7 Violet

The monument is ____.

Top Tips!

Some French colours are named after the colours of flowers and fruits. For example, 'marron' means 'chestnut', 'rose' is pink, 'orange' is orange and 'violet' is violet.

Did you know?

Sometimes, when you have a problem with your liver, your skin goes yellow. The doctors say that you are 'jaundiced'. It is like they are saying you are 'yellowed' in French! Also, when copper has been in the air a while it goes pale green, which is called 'verdigris'. 'Verd' is almost the same spelling and sound as 'vert'.

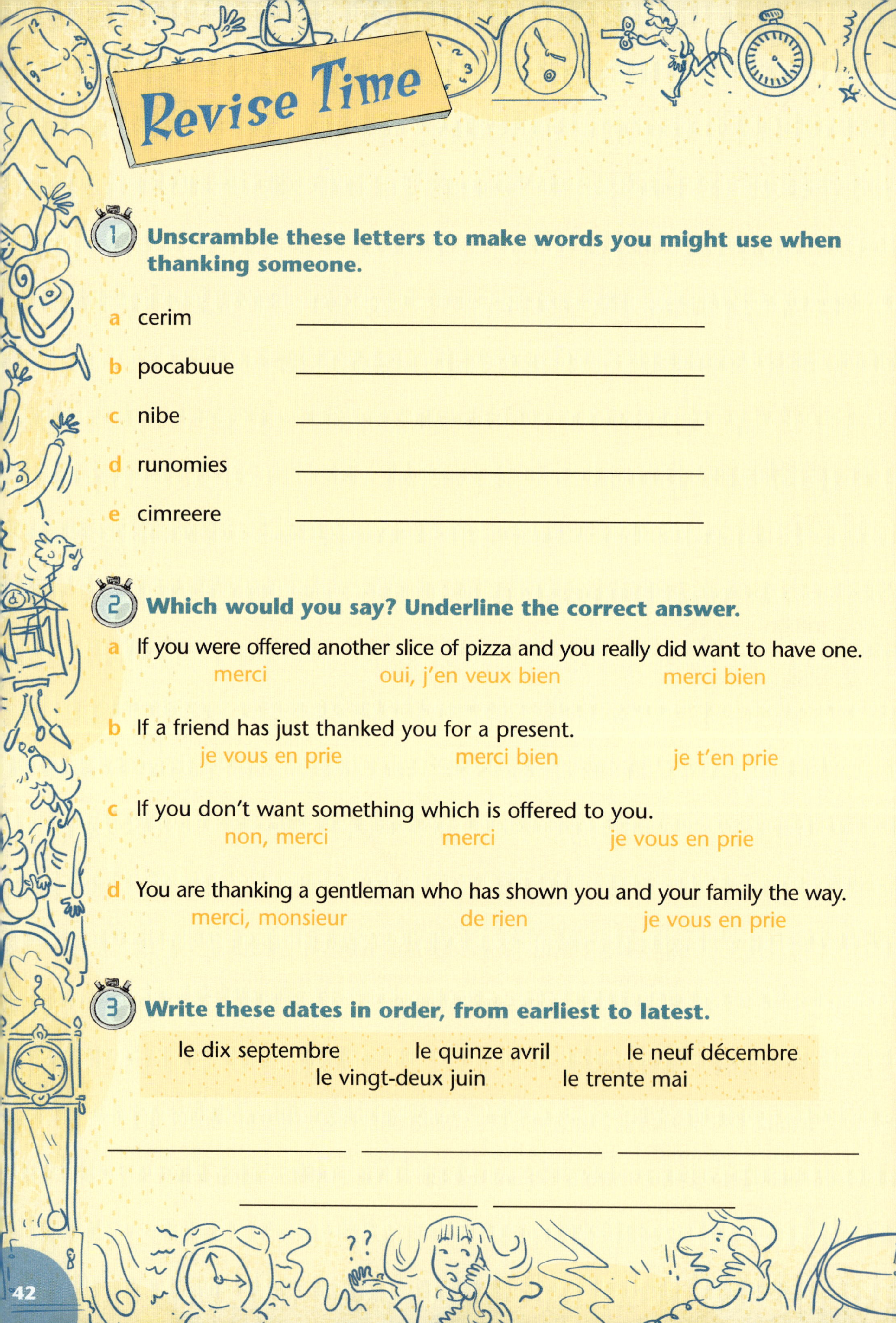

Revise Time

1 Unscramble these letters to make words you might use when thanking someone.

a cerim ______________________

b pocabuue ______________________

c nibe ______________________

d runomies ______________________

e cimreere ______________________

2 Which would you say? Underline the correct answer.

a If you were offered another slice of pizza and you really did want to have one.
merci   oui, j'en veux bien   merci bien

b If a friend has just thanked you for a present.
je vous en prie   merci bien   je t'en prie

c If you don't want something which is offered to you.
non, merci   merci   je vous en prie

d You are thanking a gentleman who has shown you and your family the way.
merci, monsieur   de rien   je vous en prie

3 Write these dates in order, from earliest to latest.

le dix septembre   le quinze avril   le neuf décembre
le vingt-deux juin   le trente mai

______________________ ______________________ ______________________

______________________ ______________________

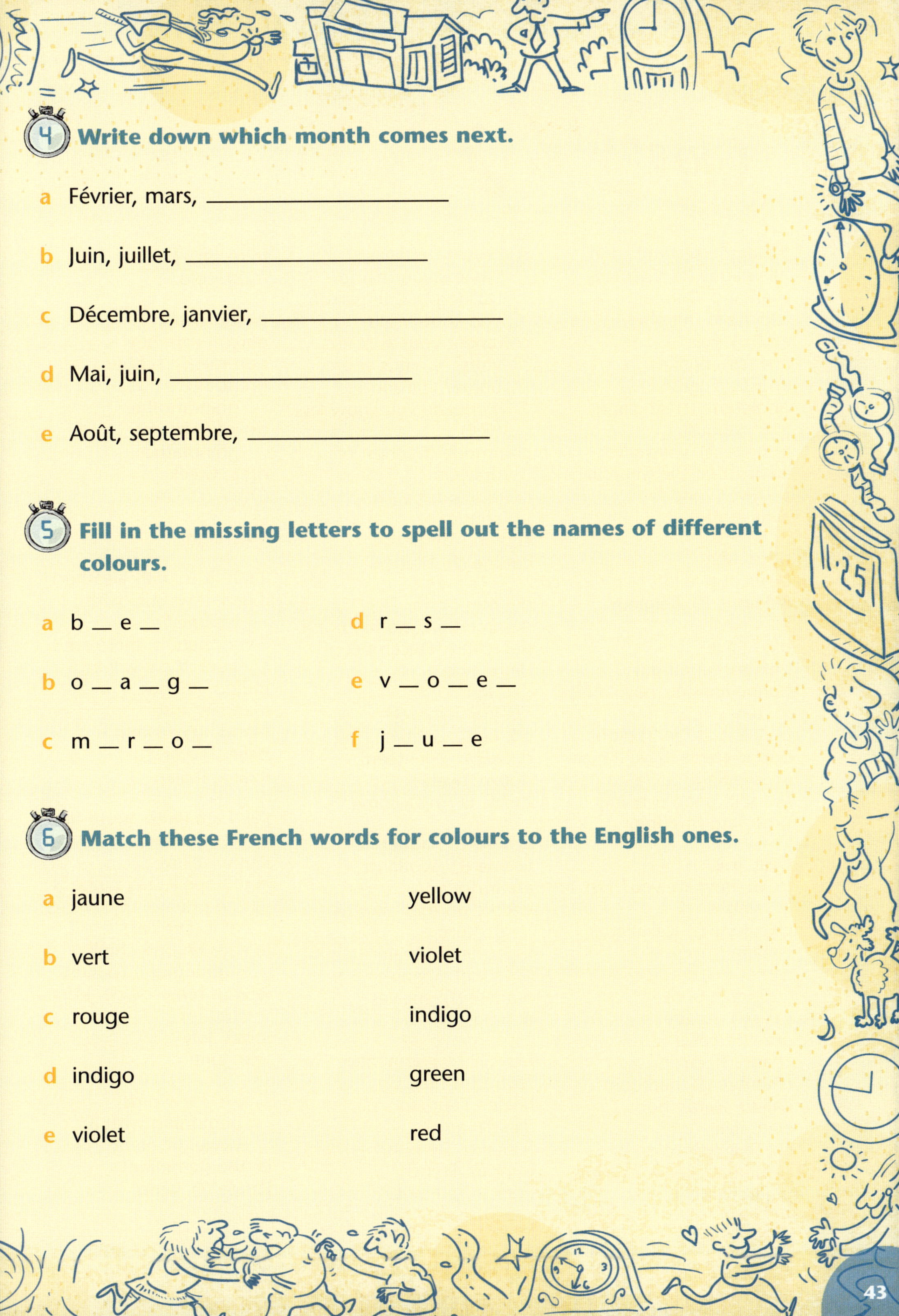

4 Write down which month comes next.

a Février, mars, ____________________

b Juin, juillet, ____________________

c Décembre, janvier, ____________________

d Mai, juin, ____________________

e Août, septembre, ____________________

5 Fill in the missing letters to spell out the names of different colours.

a b _ e _

b o _ a _ g _

c m _ r _ o _

d r _ s _

e v _ o _ e _

f j _ u _ e

6 Match these French words for colours to the English ones.

a jaune	yellow
b vert	violet
c rouge	indigo
d indigo	green
e violet	red

Glossary

à bientôt see you soon
Allemagne (f) Germany
allemand German
allô hello (on phone)
an (m) year
âne (m) donkey
anglais English
Angleterre (f) England
août August
armoire (f) wardrobe
au in/to/at the (masculine)
au revoir goodbye
avril april

beau fine
beaucoup a lot
Belgique (f) Belgium
bien well
bleu blue
bonjour good day
bonne journée have a nice day
bonne nuit good night
bonne soirée have a nice evening
bonsoir good evening
brouillard (m) fog

c'est it is
ça va how are you?/I'm alright
calculette (f) calculator
canapé (m) sofa
carnet (m) de croquis sketch book
case (f) square
cave (f) cellar
chaise (f) chair
chambre (f) bedroom
chaud warm, hot
cinq five
classeur (m) folder
comment allez-vous How are you?
comment t'appelles-tu? what is your name? (talking to one person you know well)
comment vous appelez-vous? what is your name? (Talking to someone you know less well)
commode (f) chest of drawers
cousin/cousine (m/f) cousin
crayon (m) pencil
cuisine (f) kitchen

de of
de rien think nothing of it
décembre December
deux two
dix ten
dix-huit eighteen
dix-neuf nineteen
dix-sept seventeen
douze twelve
du/de la (m/f) some

échelle (f) ladder
Écosse (f) Scotland
en in/to
encore un tour another go/turn
Espagne (f) Spain
espagnol Spanish
étagère (f) shelves
et and

fauteuil (m) armchair
feutre (m) felt tip
février February
fille (f) girl
flamand Flemish
français French
France (f) France
frère (m) brother
froid cold

gallois Welsh
garçon (m) boy
gomme (f) rubber
grand-mère (f) grandmother
grand-père (m) grandfather
grec Greek
Grèce (f) Greece

huit eight

il fait it is (with weather)
il fera it will be (with weather)
il y a there is, there are
il y aura there will be
indigo indigo
irlandais Irish
Irlande (f) Ireland
Italie (f) Italy
italien Italian

j'ai I am (with age)/I have
janvier January
jaune yellow
je m'appelle my name is
je t'en prie think nothing of it (familiar)
je vous en prie think nothing of it (polite)
je vous remercie de I thank you for
juillet July
juin June

l' the (for words beginning with a vowel or silent 'h')
la the (feminine)
lampe (f) lamp

le the (masculine)
lit (m) bed
Luxembourg (m) Luxemburg
luxembourgeois luxemburgish

mai May
mars March
mauvais bad
merci thank you
mère (f) mother
moi me
monsieur Mr/sir

néerlandais Dutch
neiger to snow
neuf nine
novembre November
numéro number

octobre October
oncle (m) uncle
onze eleven
orage (m) storm
orange orange

partout everywhere
Pays (m) Bas Holland
Pays (m) de Galles Wales
père (m) father
petit chou little one
pleut à verse pouring
pleuvoir to rain
portugais Portuguese
Portugal (m) Portugal
pour for
presque almost

quatorze fourteen
quatre four
quel âge as-tu? How old are you?
quinze fifteen

règle (f) ruler
rouge red

salle (f) à manger dining room
salle (f) de bains bathroom
salon (m) lounge
salut hello
seize sixteen
sept seven
septembre September
serpent (m) snake
ses his/her (plural)
six six
sœur (f) sister
soleil (m) sun
stylo (m) pen
Suisse (f) Switzerland

table (f) table
tante (f) aunt
treize thirteen
trente thirty
trente et un thirty-one
très very
trois three

un a/an (masculine) / one
une a/an (feminine) / one

vent (m) wind
vert green
vingt twenty
vingt et un twenty-one
violet violet
vous you (more than one person, or one person whom you don't know well)

Feminine/Masculine
All French nouns (naming words) are either masculine or feminine. Therefore, instead of saying 'it', you say 'he' ('il') or 'she' ('elle'). It is important to know whether a word is masculine or feminine, so that you know the right word to use for 'the' ('le' or 'la'), 'a' ('un' or 'une'), 'my' ('mon' or 'ma') and 'his' or 'her' ('son' or 'sa').

All the nouns in this glossary are marked with 'f' feminine or 'm' masculine.

Plural This means more than one. Remember you use a different word for 'some' ('des'), 'the' ('les'), 'my' ('mes') and 'his' and 'her' ('ses').

As you learn more French, you will see how important it is to know the masculine, feminine and plural forms of words, which go with nouns.

Vowel the letters a, e, i, o, u

Answers

Page 5

Page 7

The Witherbottoms' new neighbour asks Isabella how she is, "Ça va?"

Isabella replies to her, "Ça va bien, merci, et vous?"

Isabella asks the man next door how he is, "Comment allez-vous?"

Isabella's best friend asks how she is, "Ça va?"

Isabella replies to her best friend, "Ca va bien, merci, et toi?"

Page 9

"Comment t'appelles-tu?" Max asks the little boy standing on the doorstep.

An aeroplane is flying overhead and the boy does not hear Max properly.

"Comment t'appelles-tu?" asks Max again, as a delivery van brakes noisily on the gravel drive.

He repeats the question.

"Comment t'appelles-tu?" The little boy understands at last.

"Je m'appelle Alexandre," he replies, but now Max can't hear every word the visitor says, as Spotless starts to bark.

"Je m'appelle Alexandre!" shouts the little boy.

Suddenly, Max realises what the boy has said.

Who has come to visit? Alexandre.

Pages 10–11 Revision exercises

Exercise 1

a salut
b bonjour
c bonne nuit
d à bientôt
e au revoir

Exercise 2

a Allô
b Bonjour
c Bonne nuit
d Salut

Exercise 3

a Comment allez-vous?
b Très bien, merci, et vous?
c Ça va?
d Ça va, merci, et toi?
e Ça va, mon petit chou?

Exercise 4

Comment allez-vous?
Ça va, merci, et vous?
Ça va?
Ça va, merci, et toi?
Ça va.

Exercise 5

a, c, e

Exercise 6

Bonjour.
Je m'appelle Isabella.
Comment vous appelez-vous?
Je m'appelle Madame Dupont.

Page 13

The bottles spell 'LA LIMONADE'

Page 15

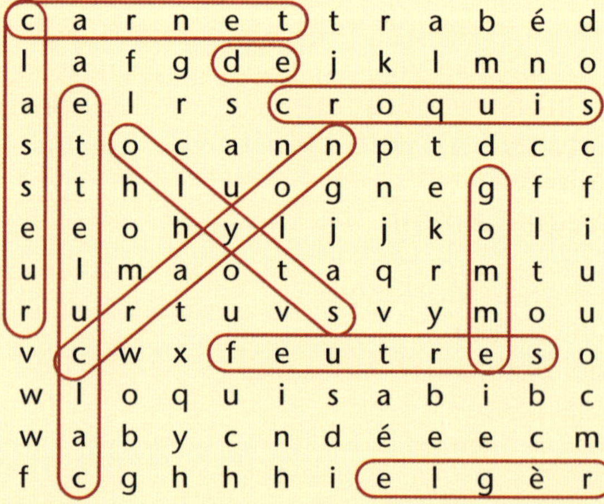

c	a	r	n	e	t	t	r	a	b	é	d
l	a	f	g	d	e	j	k	l	m	n	o
a	e	l	r	s	c	r	o	q	u	i	s
s	t	o	c	a	n	n	p	t	d	c	c
s	t	h	l	u	o	g	n	e	g	f	f
e	e	o	h	y	l	j	j	k	o	l	i
u	l	m	a	o	t	a	q	r	m	t	u
r	u	r	t	u	v	s	v	y	m	o	u
v	c	w	x	f	e	u	t	r	e	s	o
w	l	o	q	u	i	s	a	b	i	b	c
w	a	b	y	c	n	d	é	e	e	c	m
f	c	g	h	h	h	i	e	l	g	è	r

Page 17

Pierre – pour un garçon de 9 ans
Marie – pour une fille de 6 ans
Marc – pour un garçon de 10 ans
Antoine – pour un garçon de 5 ans
Chantale – pour une fille de 4 ans
Annette – pour une fille de 7 ans

Pages 18–19 Revision exercises

Exercise 1

a deux – 2
b trois – 3
c neuf – 9
d dix – 10
e sept – 7
f cinq – 5

Exercise 2

a un
b huit
c six
d quatre
e dix
f trois

Exercise 3

a stylo
b règle
c carnet de croquis
d crayon
e feutres
f gomme

Exercise 4

mon	**ma**	**mes**
classeur	calculette	feutres
stylo	gomme	crayons
carnet		

Exercise 5

a Quel âge as-tu?
b J'ai sept ans
c J'ai (number of your age here) ans.

Exercise 6

a six
b five

Page 21

Les deux fauteuils? – Dans le salon.
La table? – Dans la cuisine.
Les trois chaises? – Dans la cuisine.
La lampe? – Dans la salle à manger.
Le lit? – Dans la chambre de Mademoiselle.
La commode? – Dans la chambre de Monsieur.
L'armoire? – Dans la chambre de Monsieur.
L'étagère? – Dans la salle à manger.

Page 23

Allemagne – allemand
Italie – italien
Écosse – anglais
Espagne – espagnol
Portugal – portugais

Page 25

You would end up at number 27.

Pages 26–27 Revision exercises

Exercise 1

a bedroom
b dining room
c cellar
d bathroom
e kitchen

Exercise 2

a fauteuil
b table
c chaise
d commode
e armoire

Exercise 3

a Scotland
b Spain
c Switzerland
d Wales
e Germany

Exercise 4

a vrai
b vrai
c faux
d faux
e faux

Exercise 5

a 11 – onze
b 14 – quatorze
c 20 – vingt
d 26 – vingt-six
e 31 – trente et un

Exercise 6

a onze
b quinze
c dix-neuf
d vingt-trois
e vingt-sept
f trente et un

Page 29

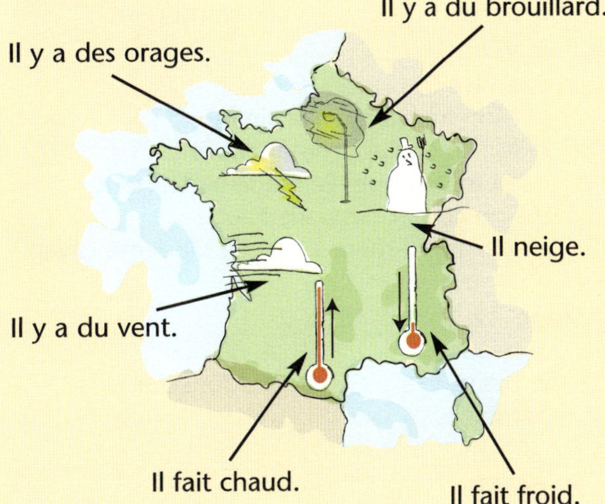

Page 31

1 Pierre Dupont
2 Antoine Leclerc
3 Marie Jamelle
4 Suzanne Degaulle
5 Marc Duval
6 Jeanne Legrand

Page 33

1 Pierre
2 Martin
3 Marianne
4 Annette
5 Yvette

Pages 34–35 Revision exercises

Exercise 1

a Il fait beau.
b Il y a du soleil.
c Il pleut.
d Il y aura du vent.
e Il fera chaud.

Exercise 2

a It is hot – Il fait chaud.
b It will be fine – Il fera beau.
c It is windy – Il fait du vent.
d It will be foggy – Il y aura du brouillard.

Exercise 3

a Isabella
b Spotless
c Max
d Sir Ralph

Exercise 4

a ah bay say day euh ABCDE
b oo vay dooblavay icks ee greck zed UVWXYZ
c coo air ess tay oo QRSTU
d eff jay ash ee jee FGHIJ
e kah ell emm enn oh KLMNO

Exercise 5

a mère
b père
c frère
d sœur
e grand-père

Exercise 6

a Mon frère s'appelle Simon.
b Ma sœur s'appelle Annette.
c Sa mère s'appelle Madame Dupont.
d Son cousin s'appelle Paul.
e Ma grand-mère s'appelle Madame Laval.

Page 37

1 beaucoup
2 bien
3 merci
4 de rien
5 Monsieur

Page 39

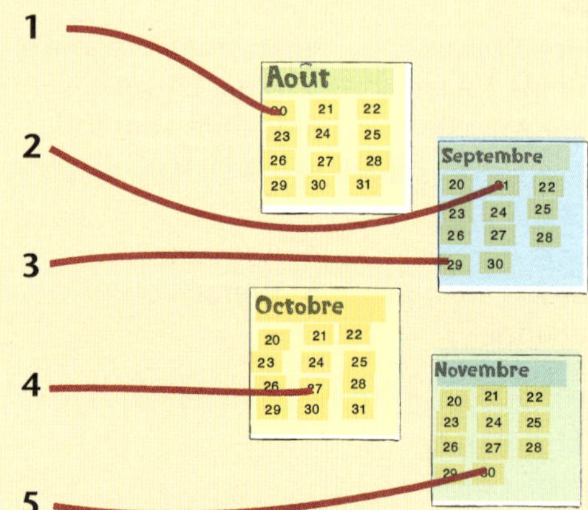

Page 41

It is a picture of the Eiffel Tower.

Pages 42–43 Revision exercises

Exercise 1

a merci
b beaucoup
c bien
d monsieur
e remercie

Exercise 2

a oui, j'en veux bien
b je t'en prie
c non, merci
d merci, monsieur

Exercise 3

le quinze avril, le trente mai, le vingt-deux juin, le dix septembre, le neuf décembre

Exercise 4

a avril
b août
c février
d juillet
e octobre

Exercise 5

a bleu
b orange
c marron
d rose
e violet
f jaune

Exercise 6

a jaune – yellow
b vert – green
c rouge – red
d indigo – indigo
e violet – violet